NEVER-THE-

Less Faith

ILENE ROWSER

ISBN 978-1-0980-5916-3 (paperback)
ISBN 978-1-0980-5917-0 (digital)

Christian Faith Publishing, Inc.
832 Park Avenue
Meadville, PA 16335
www.christianfaithpublishing.com

Scriptures marked KJV are taken from the KING JAMES VERSION (KJV)

Printed in the United States of America

Introduction

Never-the-Less Faith allow these words to soak in. How do I say thanks? Where do I begin? Everyone who inspired, encouraged, and pushed me to undertake this project, I say thanks. You know who you are and I am truly grateful.

Contents

Nevertheless Faith

Nevertheless at thy word I
will let down the net.
—Luke 5:5b

When Jesus was recruiting disciples, Simon and Andrew were casting their net. They had toiled all night long but hadn't caught anything yet.

Dropping their net, at Jesus' request, they heeded his command. Through this simple act of faith, something happened that they hadn't planned.

A miracle indeed took place, oh what these men must have thought—when the net became so full it broke, from all the fish they caught.

Nevertheless faith is trusting God when it doesn't quite make sense. It's taking Him at His word, believing He will come to your defense.

Now there's a message behind this story, one that should be addressed. Christians must have that "nevertheless" faith—if we expect to be blessed!

Storms of Life

And He arose, and rebuked the wind,
and said unto the sea, Peace, be still.
—Mark 4:39a

When the disciples were out on the sea, they were overcome with fear. Troubled by the winds blowing—despite the fact that Jesus was near.

Can't you see us as Christians, we're very much like that today? Fearful of our storms, knowing God is just a prayer away.

Instead of focusing on him, we tend to focus on our problem. Knowing God is the only one who is able to solve them.

So in the midst of your storm, just know that God will calm your raging spirit and say to your storm—peace, be still!

Rise Above

Forgetting those things which are
behind, and reaching forth unto
those things which are before.
—Philippians 3:13b

Rise above past mistakes or present circumstances. Realizing we serve a merciful God, who allows second chances.

Rise above negativity because it damages our self-esteem. Listening to negative people will make you lose sight of your dream.

Rise above the dangers of sin and Satan's powerful hold. Rise to a new way of living and watch your spiritual blessings unfold.

Rise above all manner of sickness, every ache, pain, or bad feeling. Rise to a renewed state of mind, and claim your divine healing!

Rise above.

God Is...

For there is one God; and there
is none other but He.
—Mark 12:32b

Great physician, the sacrificial lamb, rock of ages, He's the
great "I am."

Our refuge and strength during times of distress, He's also a
strong tower and a mighty fortress.

Divine creator, the chief cornerstone, He's the good shepherd—who never leaves us to walk alone.

Israelite's deliverer, a rock in a weary land, He holds the world
in the palm of His hand.

Savior, everlasting father, who hears our every call. Last but
not least—He's our all in all!

Why Worry?

Be careful for nothing; but in
everything by prayer and supplication
with thanksgiving let your requests
be made known unto God.
—Philippians 4:6

If there's something you need from the Lord, make your requests known. For if God feeds the little birds, He will take care of His own. We tend to worry over things, for which we have no control. How high on your list of priorities does faith play a role? We say, "I Will Trust in the Lord," but trust only as far as the eye can see. We sing "Think of His Goodness" and complain constantly. We say, "Lord, You've Been Good," but during the rough times, we seem to forget. We sing "I Know the Lord Will Make a Way," and wonder if our needs will be met. Now the key to true happiness—and the joy to successful living—is to be anxious for nothing and have a spirit of prayer and thanksgiving!

Courage

If God be for us, who can be against us?
—Romans 8:31b

Certainly there are times we want to give in to fear.

Overwhelming circumstances cause us not to always think clear.

Understand the world is watching how Christians react when there's a problem.

Remember, if God be for us, then we know that He can solve them.

And when the enemy makes his attack, remember God is in control.

Give your concerns to the Master, your heart, He will console.

Especially during those times we feel we can't go on, God reassures us we're not in this fight alone!

Press On

Daughter, be of good comfort; thy faith
hath made thee whole. And the woman
was made whole from that hour.
—Matthew 9:22b

The woman with an issue of blood set out on a mission. She felt if she could get close to Jesus, He could heal her condition.

For twelve long years, this ailment she endured. Despite seeing several physicians, she still had not been cured.

She pressed through the crowd as a matter of fact. Touching the hem of Jesus' garment, she made a great impact. She was made whole—at that very hour. What an awesome display of God's divine power!

Now sometimes it seems, we must press our way through. Those times when we've done all we know to do. Deliverance will come, you can expect your blessing. Don't you dare give up—you've got to keep on pressing!

The Christian Race

Let us lay aside every weight, and
the sin which doth so easily beset
us, and let us run with patience
the race that is set before us.
—Hebrews 12:1b

The Christian race is the only race where speed and ability does not determine our fate. Like in all races, on a daily basis, we must lay aside any unnecessary weight. Put on the whole armor of God, we must be equipped with the right gear. Pull off the weight of worry, and never give in to fear. Put on the armor of perseverance, it's important to remain steadfast. Pull off the weight of pride, or in this race you will not last. Put on the armor of patience, along with faith and determination. Pull off the weight of doubt, in order to reach your destination. Put on the armor of prayer because if this race is to be won, we must lay aside every weight or sin—and be willing to run!

God's Army

Be ye steadfast, unmovable, always
abounding in the work of the Lord.
—1 Corinthians 15:58b

The Christian army recruits soldiers to fight on the battlefield. The Word of God is each soldier's helmet, gun, and shield.

Jesus is our secretary of defense. God is our commander in chief. Just knowing we're on the winning side is such a great relief.

Spiritual boot camp trains us to fight Satan, our enemy. It takes discipline and dedication to become the soldier God wants us to be.

When we're in the "line of fire," we must watch as well as pray. The fringe benefits are "out of this world" once we retire someday.

Now the spiritual war department of Heaven is looking for a few good men—

Who will not go AWOL in the heat of battle—steadfastness is required to win!

Spiritual Fitness

For bodily exercise profiteth little: but
godliness is profitable unto all things,
having promise of the life that now
is, and of that which is to come.
—1 Timothy 4:8

Our society is concerned with being physically fit—but what about the soul? We've learned to exercise and how to eat right, but our spiritual lives are out of control.

We must learn to walk by faith, walk upright, walk with the Lord each day. Lift our eyes unto the hills, lift our voices with praise and with lifted hearts, we should always pray.

Run with patience, run and not be weary, run this race that the prize you may obtain. When we exercise faith and godliness, there's so much spiritually we stand to gain.

Now, the work of God gives instructions for our spiritual diet plan. Give your mind, body, and soul a spiritual workout—nourish your inner man!

A Christian Recipe

But the fruit of the spirit is
love, joy, peace, longsuffering,
gentleness, goodness, faith,
Meekness, temperance…
—Galatians 5:22–23a

There are some very special ingredients you see that have the makings of a good Christian recipe. Start with the fruit of the spirit for a recipe guaranteed not to fail. Combine the following ingredients in just the right amount. After each addition, be sure to mix well. Marinate in the Word of God, simmer with prayer and meditation. Sprinkle your words with kindness—and season your conversation. Stir in Christ-like behavior—sift out any pride or jealousy. Fold in continuous praise and worship as you become what God wants you to be. Mix generous amounts of faithfulness, for it will pay off in the long run. Prepare to serve with holiness and humility until God, the master chef, says, "Well done!"

Prayer

And all things whatsoever ye shall ask
in prayer, believing, ye shall receive.
　　　　　　　　—Matthew 21:22

*P*ositive results happen when we go to God in prayer.

*R*ealizing upon Him, we can cast every care.

*A*ll things are possible if we just believe.

*Y*ou see, whatever we ask in faith, if it's in God's will, we shall
　　receive.

*E*very trap the enemy sets can become a trapeze.

*R*emember, much can be accomplished when we go down on
　　our knees!

Be Still

Be still, and know that I am God...
—Psalm 46:10b

Be still and know that I am God, simply do as He commands—or face the uncertain consequences when we take matters into our hands.

Focus the mind on being still when everything around us seems hectic because we live in a society where getting things right now is expected.

For you see, God with His divine wisdom knows what lies ahead. Don't rely on your strength and knowledge—but rather trust Him instead.

God works in mysterious ways, and His timing may seem odd—but we must learn to just be still and allow God to be God!

Trust in the Lord

Trust in the Lord with all thine
heart; and lean not unto thine
own understanding. In all thy
ways acknowledge Him, and
He shall direct thy paths.
                —Proverbs 3:5–6

We must learn to trust God, and not lean to what we feel is right. By acknowledging Him in all our ways, we are doing what is pleasing in His sight. If we lean to our own understanding, we set ourselves up to fail. When faced with life's storms, we become like a ship that's missing the sail. Daily as we seek the Lord for guidance, if we are sincere, He will lead us through life's valleys—his course of direction will be made clear. Yes, we must learn to trust God when His ways we cannot trace. When God is Lord of our lives, we have our priorities in the right place!

Keep the Faith

Doubt says, "I can't make it. Lord, what am I going to do?"
Fear says, "I just can't take it. I'm stressed and worried too."
Hope says, "Don't give up, despite what I'm going through."
Faith says, "No matter what, Lord, I'll trust you!"

Lessons of Life

For I have learned, in whatsoever
state I am, therewith to be content.
—Philippians 4:11b

If we can see through weary eyes and keep our minds focused on the prize, we will begin to truly realize what it means to have *hope*.

If we can take everything to God in prayer, trusting upon Him, we can cast every care, then we become fully aware of what it means to have *faith*.

If your bills are due and your money is spent, yet in spite of your troubles, you can still be content. You will have learned what is meant by having real *joy*.

If you can do a good deed and not be concerned, whether or not the favor is returned, the lesson in life you will have learned is how to show *compassion*.

Through every loss, if we can see the gain, enduring heartache as well as pain, realizing in life there must be sunshine and rain, then we've learned the meaning of *tolerance*.

The Measure of a Man

For what is a man profited if
he shall gain the whole world,
and shall lose his own soul?
—Matthew 16:26

The amount of money a man has society determines as being his worth. But in God's eyes, what we do for others is what counts here on earth. What does it profit a man to accumulate material gain? Anything not done for Christ's sake is all done in vain. For you see, money may afford the luxury of life's finer things. But it can never compare to the joy and peace that the Christian life brings. The search for power and the greed for money will cause the mind to corrupt. Align your standards with God's standards, and see if they measure up!

Heart Sight

So that thou incline thine ear
unto wisdom, and apply thine
heart to understanding.
—Proverbs 2:2

When we learn to see with our hearts and not just with our eyes, there's so much about life we would understand and realize.

It's the little things in life we seldom notice or fail to mention—taking them for granted, God has a way of getting our attention.

What we fail to realize, if others could choose—they would welcome the opportunity to be in our shoes.

Can we understand the needs of others if we've never been there before? Shouldn't their loss or misfortune make us appreciate what we have all the more?

So from this day forward, we should make a new start—to look at things not just by sight, but also with the heart!

Behind the Scenes

While we look not at the things which
are seen, but at the things which are
not seen: for the things which are
seen are temporal: but the things
which are not seen are eternal.
—2 Corinthians 4:18

God is working behind the scenes of my life, those areas the naked eye cannot see. He's pruning and shaping my rough places, so I might become what He wants me to be.

For my life, He designed the blueprint and has the master plan. If he can't correct the problem—then surely no one can.

Those areas headed for ruin or at the point for spiritual decay—God is repairing and replacing those things and clearing the debris away.

Allow God to work behind the scenes of your life, and soon you will find that you are becoming the person he originally had in mind!

Forgetting and Remembering

Bless the Lord, O my soul, and
forget not all His benefits.
—Psalm 103:2

Don't forget to remember the blessings God has given unto you. But remember to forget past hurts—and my failures too.

Don't forget to remember, there are brighter days ahead. But remember to forget, the negative things people have said.

Don't forget to remember that you are truly blessed. But remember to forget the times you felt worried or depressed.

One thing we should remember is to always be careful—to never forget, to always stay prayerful!

For Your Good

And we know that all things work
together for good to them that
love God, to them who are the
called according to his purpose.
—Romans 8:28

Storms are designed to strengthen the soul. No matter how they affect us, remember God is in control. We must understand that on the whole—God is working things for our good.

Storms often take us by surprise, and many times are blessings in disguise. But one thing we should not fail to realize—God is working things for our good.

So if you're waiting on a breakthrough and your deliverance seems long overdue, just know God has something great in store for you—because He's working things for your good.

God's Promises

The Lord is not slack
concerning His promise…
—2 Peter 3:9a

Throughout God's Word there are promises, for whatever you're going through. Time and time again, they have been proven to be tried and true.

Isaiah 40:31 instructs us to wait upon the Lord, our strength He will renew. James 4:7 warns us, "Resist the devil, and he will flee from you."

Matthew 17:20 challenges us to have faith the size of a mustard seed. Philippians 4:19 reminds us, my God shall supply all your need.

John 16:33 encourages us, in this world of tribulation, be of good cheer. Psalm 27:1 says, "The Lord is my light and salvation—whom shall I fear?"

James 1:12 gives the promise of a crown once we've endured being tempted and tried. Psalm 32:8 says, we have the assurance—the Lord will always be our guide.

Now search the scriptures for God's promises, you can stand upon what you've read. Because the Lord is not slack concerning His promise, and He will do just what he said!

ABCs to Live By

I can do all things through Christ
which strengtheneth me.
—Philippians 4:13

*A*lways be willing to accept who you are.
*B*elieve in yourself and you will go far.
*C*oncentrate on positive things.
*D*iscover the possibilities each new day brings.
*E*xpect some challenges, along the way.
*F*ace them with confidence each and every day.
*G*et into the habit, of saying "I can."
*H*ave faith, don't give up, stick to your plan.
*I*gnore negative comments that people tend to say.
*J*ust be determined to let nothing stand in your way.
*K*eep moving forward, don't dwell upon the past.
*L*ive each day to the fullest, as if you knew it were your last.
*M*ake it a point to eliminate stress.
*N*ow it's up to you to find your own happiness.
*O*pportunities are awaiting for you to explore.
*P*ersistence is the key that unlocks the door.
*Q*uit worrying about things for which you have no control.
*R*each for the stars and never lose sight of your goal.
*S*tand firm on what you believe.

There's no limit, when you stay focused, to what you can achieve.
Understand the importance of learning from your mistakes.
Vow to make a difference, commitment is what it takes.
We have the potential to become whatever we desire to be.
Xerox in your mind, you can make your dreams a reality.
You can achieve success once you put your mind to it.
Zero in on the fact, you must be willing to pursue it!

Stir Up the Gift

Stir up the gift of God,
which is in thee…
—2 Timothy 1:6

God has implanted within each of us a very special gift. To edify the body of Christ, encourage, and uplift. It was not given merely for worldly fortune and fame; but rather to glorify and magnify our precious Jesus' name. It matters not how small the gift may be, dedicate it to the glory of God with sincerity. Now stir up the gift, God has invested in you, and you'll find there's no limit to what God can and will do!

Stir up your gift!

Comfort Zone

For God has not given us the
spirit of fear; but of power, and
of love, and of a sound mind.
—2 Timothy 1:7

It seems no matter how hard we try, it's very difficult sometimes to test our wings and fly. There's always a chance of failure and fear of the unknown. Things just seem less complicated when we're in our comfort zone. But like the eagle, we have to "stir our nest." Take off with faith, and pray we're doing what's best. You never know what you can accomplish until you give it a try. Don't sit too long daydreaming—or life will surely pass you by. People will try to discourage you because they simply don't understand. Never give in to their negative comments, allowing Satan the upper hand. Your spirit will become restless when it's time to move on. Never settle for less than the best—be willing to leave your comfort zone!

The Cost of Salvation

Who His own self bare our sins
in His own body on the tree…
1 Peter 2:24a

For our sins Jesus paid an awesome price. He offered Himself as a human sacrifice. Before we take it lightly, we must think twice—*was Jesus dying worth it to you?*

"Hosanna, Hosanna," the people cried. Days later the crowd said He should be crucified. In Pilate's court, Jesus was tried—*was Jesus dying worth it to you?*

Convicted, Jesus endured the agony and shame. "Father forgive then," choosing not to place the blame. Jesus fulfilled the mission for which He came—*was Jesus dying worth it to you?*

Sometimes I wonder why He chose to die for someone so underserving as you and I. Show by example in everything you do that Jesus dying was worth it to you!

The Master's Touch

They that are whole have no need of
a physician, but they that are sick:
I came not to call the righteous,
but sinners to repentance.
—Mark 2:17b

There's something special, about the master's touch. He can take very little and turn it into much. He performed many miracles, opened eyes that were blind. Healing the sick, raising the dead—He ministered to all mankind. He made the lame walk and cured men of leprosy. He broke Sabbath laws, creating much publicity. He cast out demons and healed a withered hand. So much about the master, people didn't understand. Having dealings with sinners, Jesus stood accused. Common ordinary people were the ones He used. Now just in case, you've had a poor start, at this very moment, you can give Jesus your heart. The first requirement is to repent of your sin. For He's the only one who can make you whole again. A life dedicated to Christ is one that is sweet. Just one touch from the master will make your life complete!

Praise Your Way Through

I will bless the Lord at all times: His
praise shall continually be in my mouth.
—Psalm 34:1

Does it ever seem your faith is on trial? Sometimes you
want to give up and just throw in the towel. This message
was meant especially for you. In the midst of trying times,
learn to praise your way through.

When it seems your problems are ever increasing, the
Word of God reminds us to pray without ceasing. There's
one other thing you should do, when your back's against the
wall—just praise your way through.

Now, in everything, give thanks, rejoice in the Lord
always. The key to your deliverance is in your praise. Satan
wants to steal your joy and your testimony too. So just stomp
him under your feet and praise your way through!

Our Troubled Hearts

Let not your heart be troubled:
ye believe in God, believe also in me.
—John 14:1

Why should our hearts be troubled when God is always near? Because He is our refuge and strength, we have no need to fear.

Why should our hearts be troubled? Acknowledge Him in all our ways. In the midst of our troubles, we must keep giving God the praise.

Why should our hearts be troubled when our strongest weapon is prayer? We can cast every burden upon Him and, in faith, leave it there.

Yes, why should our hearts be troubled? God's promises are true. He will never leave nor forsake us—there's nothing He won't see you through!

Look to the "Son"

I will lift up mine eyes unto hills,
from whence cometh my help.
—Psalm 121:1

Have your once blue skies suddenly turned to gray? Are you faced with problems and find it hard to pray? Don't give up as if Satan has won, just keep your focus upward—and look to the Son.

Don't sit around worrying about your situation. Doing so will cause you pain and frustration. Your first step to deliverance will have just begun—when you take the time to look to the Son.

Now if it seems you're at the end of your rope, the cares of this world makes you feel you just can't cope. You can call up Heaven, spiritually dial 911, your hope will be renewed—once you look to the Son!

At the Point of Your Need

The Lord is my shepherd;
I shall not want.
—Psalm 23:1

Spiritually, are you at an all-time low? Standing at a crossroad, wondering which way to go? Have a talk with God before you proceed, for He will meet you at the point of your need.

Is there something from the Lord you truly desire? Satan says it is impossible, but remember he is a liar. With God all things are possible, just take heed that God will meet you at the point of your need.

Now go to the Word of God and see what He has to say. In due time He will answer, so just continue to pray. Watch God work things out as He takes the lead to meet you at the point of your need!

Broken Vessels

...He shall be a vessel unto honor,
sanctified, and meet for the master's use,
and prepared unto every good work.
—2 Timothy 2:21b

As humans, like pottery, we too are made of clay. And sometimes from life's pressures, we become broken along the way.

Broken dreams, broken relationships, some hurts go unspoken—because the pain runs deep from being cracked and broken.

But it really does not matter what shape you may be in—God, the master craftsman, can make you whole again.

So give God those broken pieces, on Him cast every care—for He can mend a broken life that seems shattered beyond repair!

Live in the Now

Take therefore no thought for the
morrow: for the morrow shall take
thought for the things of itself.
—Matthew 6:34

Learn to live in the present, learn to live in the now. Because the future has a way of handling itself somehow. Tomorrow may never be, and yesterday is gone. This moment in time is all we have to build our lives upon. So learn to live in the now, do it without delay. Don't allow the weight of tomorrow's worries, make you lose sight of today.

Work While It's Day

I must work the works of Him that
sent me, while it is day: the night
cometh, when no man can work.
—John 9:4

Each day of our lives is like a blank check, God gives with the intent—within the next twenty-four hours, our time will be well spent.

Imprinted on each check is today's date. So don't try to cash it tomorrow, for it will be too late.

On the pay to the order line, each name is addressed. Because it's signed in the name of Jesus, He can handle any need or request.

Each check has a number, representing our days are numbered too. You see, God is keeping a record of everything we do.

So work while it is day, make it one of your top concerns. And you will have no regrets, when the Lord returns!

Live Your Life

Let your light so shine before men, that
they may see your good works, and
glorify your Father which is in heaven.
—Matthew 5:16

Live your life so others will know that you have passed
this way. May the love of Christ be demonstrated in everything you do and say.

For it's not how long you live, but what matters is how
well. The fact that you're a Christian—others should be able
to tell.

Some people may never read the Bible but will read
your life instead. Be careful of the message you send so others
are not misled.

Each day is like the pages of a book that reveals our
life's story. So live your life in such a way that God will get
the glory.

Transformation

We can transform our lives once we transform our way of thinking. Look back at life with appreciation, look forward to the future with anticipation. Look back and learn to forgive and forget. Look forward without any remorse or regret. Look back and thank God for His faithfulness. Look forward with heartfelt gratefulness. Look back and abandon anxiety. Look forward and embrace positivity. Look back and eliminate stress. Look forward and give God our very best. Look back and see how far we've come. Look forward to the one our help comes from.

Butterfly

The butterfly's journey begins as a caterpillar enclosed in a cocoon. A slow process one of which it mustn't emerge too soon. Struggling to release itself imagine of all things, the struggle is what strengthens its wings. I'm sure the caterpillar grew tired enduring all of this, but it was being transformed into a butterfly through the process of metamorphosis. As humans, we too transform through our personal metamorphosis struggling and feeling, "Lord, how much more of this?" We must be mindful our wings of faith are being strengthened, so like the butterfly we too might soar to heights we've never reached before. Allow God to perfect His work within you by trusting His process. There's always a price and a sacrifice that comes with achieving success.

Breakthrough

Breakthrough—those hours between midnight and daybreak. Those minutes between dusk and dawn, those seconds between dawn and daylight. It's during our dark times we may want to give up and give in, but in the midst of our doubts and fears, those times we have to struggle to fight back tears; those times when Satan seems to have the upper hand, we must trust God has a greater plan.

Grace Unexpected

Unexpected grace when despite our best intentions is favor we cannot or did not earn. It's when God shows mercy instead of judgment that seems cruel, harsh, and stern. In the midst of our failures, He shows compassion as He takes the lead, not to severely punish, but instead minister to our need. There are times we make mistakes and feel sorrow and regret, but our loving Father extends grace in ways we least expect. So when life seems to throw you one fast curve—praise God for the times we receive better than we deserve.

A Clean Heart

Create within me a clean heart, renew the right spirit within me. Make me over, Lord, into the person you would have me to be. Cleanse my heart and mind, wash me through and through so that I might become an humble servant that reflects the heart of you. In Jesus' name. Amen.

Our Awesome God

God is an awesome God who has the capability of becoming whatever we need Him to be. There are many adjectives to describe Him and He wears each title well. He's such a great God who can do anything but fail. I am... because—God is.

Seize the Moment

Seize the moment with great confidence and authority. Tomorrow is not promised. Take advantage of every opportunity.

Seize the moment. Life shouldn't just pass you by,
Think of the remorse, if you don't stay the course,
And at the very least, give it a try.

Thank You, Lord

Thank you, Lord, for being patient and never giving up on me. Thank you for your long-suffering and showing love unconditionally. Thank you for the times we've broken your heart, yet you extended your loving touch. You went to Calvary to die for our sins because you loved us just that much. Thank you, Lord, for keeping us when times were tough. For protecting us from dangers seen and unseen—Lord, we can't thank you enough.

Our Dreams

There's something within us that is strong beyond measure. A precious jewel awaiting to be unearthed like a hidden treasure. This is a perfect example of what our dreams are made of, precious Gifts from God above. A thought, an idea is where our dream starts. It then takes root and grows deep within our hearts. Nurture and develop your dreams, don't just let them die. You've got to believe in yourself and at least give it a try. Seek guidance in planning, make your vision clear. Never allow anything and anyone cause you to give in to fear. No matter how strange to others it seems, don't you dare give up on your dreams.

Write the Vision

Write the vision and make it plain. Think of what you stand to gain. Write the vision because it plays a vital role when we take the time to outline each goal. Write the vision, don't allow your dreams to die. You must be willing to at least give it a try. Write the vision and follow through; as it unfolds, your dreams will come true.

Change

We look at our lives and wonder why we're in the predicament that we're in. We say things need to change but don't know how or where to begin. Making positive changes is necessary—and it starts in the mind. Toxic people and negative situations must be left behind. What's not normal or routine becomes comfortable, it's so easy to complain. We tend to take on unhealthy habits, which temporarily numbs the pain. The holding pattern can leave us terrified between a rock and a hard place. It's easier to deal with what's familiar than the reality we need to face. If you want there to be a change in your life, find the courage somehow to say enough is enough—the time to do it is right *now*.

Renewed

When the pressures of life seem to have taken its toll, it's hard to focus on the fact that God is in control. I may be broken and battered but with heartfelt gratitude on the path to wholeness, I am being renewed. During times of tribulation, Lord, I look to You for consolation. I try to focus on remaining calm and subdued as my faith is strengthened, I'm being renewed. When my trust has been shaken to the core, and it seems I can't handle the stress anymore, with a made-up mind and the right attitude—I am encouraged because I'm being renewed.

Restoration

We may give up on ourselves, but God never gives up on us. The fact He loves us unconditionally is a plus. He's aware of our faults and failures yet still loves us no doubt. He sees our potential when others count us out. Those areas that seem shattered beyond repair, "I've been healed and set free" is what we'll be able to declare. Life can leave us battered, feeling defeated, and broken. Some hurts too often go unspoken. Once restoration takes place, we then become brand-new and we won't look like what we've been through.

Purpose and Destiny

God has plans for our lives
Plans with purpose and destiny.
His desire is that we become
All that He wants us to be.
That goal, dream, or career move
Go ahead and pursue it.
Have faith enough to believe
That you can do it.
How many unfulfilled hopes and dreams
have been placed on hold?
How many were taken to the grave
not given a chance to unfold?
Your dreams and aspirations
do whatever you can
To bring them to fruition
The opportunity may never come again.

Blessings in Trials

There are blessings in your trials; for every dark cloud, there's a silver lining. Once the storm has passed, look forward to the sun shining. It's during our dark and lonely hours, we can't always see clear bask in the warmth of God's goodness knowing His presence is near. Didn't you see His hand in the situation when you thought you blew it? And you began to wonder and worry if you'd ever get through it? There are blessings in your trials, though you may not see it now—trust God's timing, He'll work things out somehow. So look for the blessings in your trials despite what you're going through. You very well may discover they were hidden in plain view.

Experience

The things I've experienced in life has made me who I am today. I wouldn't trade the experiences because of the lessons I've learned along the way. Experiences that have produced losses as well as gains. Experiences that have stretched me from the growing pains. In spite of it all, we must always keep a positive outlook. There are lessons in life to be learned that can't be obtained from a book. It's truly very odd and sadly strange—there are those who refuse to embrace change. We change wardrobes, outer appearances, houses, and cars; we'll settle for hanging on to old baggage nurturing hurts, old wounds, and scars. Life affords us opportunities to learn and grow. There are times you'll have to walk away and just let it go.

A Love Affair

Hello, God, it's me. He responds, "My child, I haven't heard from you lately." I can imagine those words would cut like a knife, forcing us to take a look at our prayer life. Perhaps we rush through a devotional or a scripture or two and think that we're spending quality time with you. We go to God with our wants and needs thinking we can repay Him with our good deeds. Before our meals, we say grace. But the fact remains, there are some truths we must face. God is a jealous God and at times we have the gall to treat Him like a genie at our beckoning call. Fall in love with the Lord and once you do, show Him in actions and words just how much He really means to you.

No Weapon

No weapon (evil force or evil source) formed against you (Satan may attack but God's got your back) shall prosper (Satan may think he's won but the battle has just begun). Serve, Satan, notice shoot your best shot, arm yourself with the Word of God, Satan, give it all you've got. He may seem to be winning, but it's only hit or miss. Whatever you're going through, just say and believe God's got this.

Psalm 23 Remix

The Lord is my Shepherd who supplies all my needs. He allows me to rest in green pastures and by the still waters He leads. Leading me in the path of righteousness, He restores my soul. Although I may walk through dark valleys of death—I will fear *no* evil because God's in control. Because He is with me, I am comforted by His rod and staff. It's reassuring to know God is working on my behalf. In the presence of my enemies, He prepares a table. Anoints my head with oil, my cup overflows, which lets me know He's able. Every day of my life goodness and mercy shall follow me, and I will dwell in the house of the Lord for all eternity.

If Not Now, When?

Those dreams and aspirations you have neatly tucked away. The ones you've said you'll get around to doing someday. Dreams that tug at your heartstrings every now and then. If now is not the time, do you know when? Are you afraid of moving out of your comfort zone or fearful of making mistakes? Know and believe within your heart, you have what it takes. Perhaps you may be thinking where and how do I begin. If your answer is not now, can you tell me when? Opportunity is knocking, go ahead and answer the door. Why are you hesitating, what are you waiting for? Stop making excuses. I'll ask you once again—if now is not the time, please tell me when?

Lessons from Noah's Ark

Noah was about to embark upon constructing a huge ark. *Lesson 1:* Whatever God assigns us to do, we must be willing to follow through. For forty years, Noah preached, "It's going to rain." Can you imagine how the people must have thought he was insane? *Lesson 2:* No pretense, God will instruct you to do things that doesn't quite make sense. Being onboard the ark with animals had to be an unpleasant situation. But it didn't deter Noah from reaching his destination. *Lesson 3:* It's not what you're going through, but where you're headed to. The earth became flooded by constant downpour. People wanted to enter the ark, but God locked the door. *Lesson 4:* There's a huge price to pay when we disobey. Once the rains stopped, there was a rebirth. Everything flourished when God replenished the earth. *Lesson 5:* It's true, God makes all things new. God placed a rainbow in the sky. A dove carrying an olive branch was a sign that the earth was dry. *Lesson 6:* We all will experience dark days, but just know that trouble won't last always!

Be encouraged.

Raise Your Praise

Raise the level of your praise, lift His name on high. Raise the level of your praise, tell your worries and cares goodbye. Raise the level of your praise, go ahead and give it a try. There's deliverance in your praise. Raise the level of your praise, leave your troubles behind. Raise the level of your praise, peace and contentment you will find. Raise the level of your praise and watch God blow your mind. There's a breakthrough in your praise. Raise the level of your praise, so lift up your voice. Raise the level of your praise, now let us rejoice. Raise the level of your praise, go ahead and make the right choice because there's a blessing in your praise.

Face Your Fears

Stepping out in faith requires taking that leap, moving into waters that may be uncharted and deep. There may be times you'll have to take the journey alone and make the decision to move out of your comfort zone. Satan tries to cast doubt and uncertainty; recognize it for what it is, another trick of the enemy. Be willing to put in the work, you must persevere. Be specific in your planning, make your vision clear. Expect there to be detours because things don't always go as planned. If God has placed a dream within your heart, upon His Word you can stand. Stepping out in faith takes courage—a fact you must admit. It requires hard work and determination, so don't just give up and quit.

Look on the Bright Side

There's a light at the end of the tunnel. Behind every dark cloud is a silver lining. It's always darkest before dawn to remind us the sun will soon be shining. Isn't that how life goes, filled with its highs and lows? So hold your head up, be encouraged, always look on the bright side. We can never drift too far out of God's reach even if we tried.

Peace during Our Storms

Storms come disguised in various ways and at times can put a damper on our praise. When you're feeling discouraged and your anxiety is on the increase, in the midst of your storm, God will give you peace.

We gain strength through every trial when we trust and believe it only lasts for a little while. In His due time, our trials will cease; but in the meantime, and between time, God will give you peace.

So the times when you're going through, hope is the only thing we have to hold onto. Stand on the promises of His Word and watch your worries decrease. In the midst of your storms, just know that God will give you peace.

Life's Little Things

The little things in life we must learn to appreciate. A lesson way too often we discover much too late. You can't miss what you've never had, but you can miss things once they're gone. If we find ourselves in this predicament, consider it a lesson learned and move on. Don't beat yourself up and let it get the best of you, nor waste precious time worrying about something you can't undo. Learn to appreciate life's little things because they could be gone in the batting of an eye. Don't just let them slip away and leave you wondering, "Lord, what happened and why?"

Believe

A child believes in the promise that Santa will come through. The awesome privilege of prayer is believing what God can and will do. So with childlike faith and wonder of Santa's arrival with anticipation, believe in the power of prayer with great expectation.

The Birthday Party

The banquet hall was beautifully decorated in colors of red and green. The room was simply gorgeous, it looked like a page out of a magazine. The tables were draped in white linen, candles were dimly lit. It was a night to be remembered; the party was sure to be a great hit. Balloons, streamers, confetti, and last-minute details were under way. The caterers prepared enticing foods for a huge buffet. Music was playing softly; the band was live. The party was scheduled to begin at a quarter past five. As the guests made their arrival they were waiting for the honoree. After some time of chit-chatting, they began asking where could he be? The answer soon became obvious, the conclusion was rather grim. In the midst of all the preparations, sadly no one invited Him. The moral of the story—don't get so caught up in all the festivities that we lose sight of the real reason as to why we celebrate this glorious Christmas season. Happy Birthday, Jesus!

A Gift for Jesus

A birthday gift for Jesus
now what could I possibly bring,
to someone very Dear to me, who has everything.
He's not impressed with jewels,
for He owns the silver and gold—
a gift he received, as a young child,
from the Wise Men in days of old.
It's pointless to give material things,
because the book of Psalm reveals;
the earth is the Lord's and the fullness thereof,
He owns the cattle on a thousand hills.
The best gift anyone can give,
cannot be bought and placed on a shelf.
It must be a gift that comes from within,
a gift where you give of yourself.
I want my gift to be special,
not something wrapped and placed under a tree,
but rather a gift that keeps on giving,
something personal to Him from me.
Now once we search within ourselves,
the answer will become clearer,
the only gift befitting our dear sweet Jesus
is the image reflected in the mirror.

Give Yourself to Jesus!

My Hope Lies in You

Lord, you've always been faithful, the one upon whom I can always depend. You've been with me from the beginning and will see me through until the end. Without your grace and mercy, I don't know what I would do. Which is why I can truly say, my hope lies in You.

Like David, You are my refuge and strength who's always been by my side. Under the shelter of Your wings, I can safely hide. Every test or trial I've encountered, you've always seen me through. Which is why I know, beyond a shadow of a doubt—my hope lies in You.

Praise God Anyhow

Turn your worries into worship, your problems into praise. Acknowledge God in all things, rejoice in Him always. Turn your hollers into hallelujahs, your moans into music. Satan tries to attack the mind in hopes that we will lose it. Turn your tests into testimonies is what we should do. Hold on and get ready to receive your breakthrough. God will dispatch angels, quicker than right now. So when Satan shoots his best shot—go ahead and praise God anyhow!

Lord, Where Are You?

I close my eyes and quietly bow. Lord, where are you? I need you now. The times He seems so far away is when I wonder, does He hear me when I pray? I hold on to my faith when I'm in a dark place. Lord, I sense your presence though I can't visibly see your face. I praise you in spite of what I'm going through, trusting and believing you will come to my rescue. So when God seems so close but yet so far, just know He will meet us right where we are.

Your Blessings

God can do exceedingly and abundantly above what we ask or think. Don't give up because your blessings may very well be on the brink. Sometimes we get in a hurry and want to move full steam ahead. Later to discover, we should have waited on God instead. As humans, we tend to want everything right now and pray that things will eventually work itself out—somehow. Trust God's timing and allow His blessings to unfold. Don't tie God's hand by forcing Him to place your blessings on hold.

Fruit of the Spirit Prayer

———————

Lord, teach me to show *love* and concern towards others that best represents you. May I always maintain the *joy* of the Lord despite what I may be going through. Grant me *peace*, help me realize living unhappy and depressed is such a waste. May I show *long-suffering* and patience towards others by not reacting angrily in haste. Lord, season my words with *gentleness*, being mindful of any harsh words I might say. Help me to serve others with *goodness* that honors and pleases you in every way. Lord, may I have *faith* to completely trust you and not choosing to live in fear. Grant me the spirit of *meekness* and to be humble and sincere. Lord, help me to maintain *temperance* as well as self-control. Living out the fruit of the Spirit is my daily goal.

In Jesus's name. *Amen.*

Make the Choice to Rejoice

Make the choice to rejoice although your heart may be breaking. Sometimes in our darkest place of pain a blessing is in the making. Make the choice to rejoice when the odds against you are stacked high. Those times when you want to give up and just break down and cry. Making the choice to rejoice can be the wisest thing to do. It very well may be the path that leads to your breakthrough.

Dealing with Anger

The parties involved were hurt, mad, and upset. Their body language set the tone. No one was willing to put pride aside and just leave well enough alone. Both parties had to have the first and last word because they both felt that they were right—hot, disgusted, and furious, ready to explode like a stick of dynamite. When someone's ready to shoot off at the mouth, don't supply them with a verbal bullet. When tempers become cocked in trigger mode, we shouldn't give them a reason to pull it. Learning to practice self-control certainly is the key. Take the high road, extend the olive branch or at the very least agree to disagree.

You Be You

There are those who look for the worst in us instead of focusing on the best. Always bringing up our past, never giving it a rest. When it comes to being yourself, raise the bar. Never allow others to define who you are. We may not measure up to what others expect, but we're all worthy of the utmost respect. Search within yourself because one thing is true—no one can master the art of you being you!

Our Destiny

Move forward along the path to your destiny. Do whatever it takes. Resolve to make things happen because opportunity awaits. Walk through the door towards your destiny. New adventures you're about to embark. Never stop trying when it seems you may have missed the mark. Standing at the crossroads of your destiny, there's no need to fear the unknown. Don't ever become complacent, move out of your comfort zone. Learn to embrace your destiny. Your faith and hope He will renew, with motivation and determination your dreams will come true.

Heart of God

There should be a place in our hearts where the Lord resides, where there's no room for vanity. A place where God is developing us into the person He would have us to be. A special place where we allow God to take charge of our plans. A place where we surrender as clay in the master's hands. As I seek you, Lord, for direction in all I say and do, may my heart always be a perfect reflection of You.

The Grace of God

There are some folk, if they could choose, would welcome the opportunity to be in our shoes. I can't imagine all the suffering of others, no matter how hard I try. But I say if not for the grace of God, there goes I. Some folks may not have an abundance of material wealth nor a reasonable portion of strength and health. When I see others lacking many things that money can't buy, I realize but if not for the grace of God, there goes I. Satan wants to make us feel we're not quite up to par. Don't become his victim allowing Satan to define who you are. Serve the enemy notice, don't buy into this lie. I'm convinced if not for the grace of God, there goes I.

Beauty from Ashes

Beauty can be found in the ashes of great sorrow. Offering the promise of hope for a better tomorrow. Beauty can be found in ashes because God will go to great length to provide healing and much needed strength. Beauty can be found in ashes where deep pain lies. Underneath all the dust and debris can be blessings in disguise. Beauty can be found in the ashes because once we've gone through, God cleanses and purges away any residue. Beauty can be found in the ashes once we've gone through the fire. When we allow Him to dwell within our hearts, we'll become the person He would so desire.

The Next Level

God wants to take you to the next level
But there are a few things you should know.
Some people, places, and things
You must release and let go.
Going to the next level is a process
that begins in the mind.
Negative thoughts and negative people—
you must leave behind.
There are those who won't understand
but that's okay.
Be determined to let nothing or no one stand in your way.
Don't listen to foolish talk from the Devil.
Tune him out, move along, and don't stoop to his level.
The journey won't be easy, that's for sure.
There will be growing pains you'll have to endure.
Each level are chapters along the journey
Lessons in life's education.
So persevere and keep striving—
To reach your desired destination.

Your Cares

I was overwhelmed and filled with anxiety.
I prayed, "Lord, I need your help." He said,
"Cast all your cares on me."
I gave Him my problems but kept taking them back.
I wondered why I was always stressed—
It seemed the enemy was under attack.
I said, "Lord, how can this be?"
He said, "I'm still waiting on you to cast your
cares on me." My life was in chaos
and I was such a mess. Frustrated to say the least.
When the weight of my worries began to take its toll—
I finally surrendered allowing God to take full control.
My burdens became lighter and my worries ceased.
My hope was renewed and my faith increased.
The moral of the story
Which I'm sure you will agree—
Take God at His Word when He says—
Cast all your cares upon me.

Success

Remember the story of the tortoise and the hare?

Though taunted and ridiculed, the tortoise didn't seem to care.

He moved right along at a steady pace.

Persevered and ultimately won the race.

The moral of the story, don't worry about your speed.

Faith, motivation, and determination are the tools you will need.

Set specific goals, don't settle for anything less.

The path is never easy along the road to success.

The point I'm driving home—keep your prize in view.

Never allow anything or anyone to stop or hinder you.

Prayer of Purpose

Help me, Lord, to become all that I can be.

Help me to see all you have in store for me.

Reveal Your purpose for my life, make the vision plain.

I realize when I put You first, Lord, there's so much I stand to gain.

May I follow the path, You have laid out for me.

Like Jabez's prayer, I ask that You enlarge my territory.

Lord as the vision unfolds, deliver me from any binding strong holds.

You have definite plans for my life for which I am fully aware,

To walk in my purpose is my daily prayer.

In Jesus' name—Amen

Forgiveness

I had mixed emotions, hurt, disappointed, and sad.
I said, "Lord, I need you," because I was bitter and mad.
I prayed and I cried and as tears continued to flow.
He said, "My child, I understand but you've got to let it go."
I was frustrated and visibly upset.
I thought, Lord, how could I possibly just forgive and forget.
He spoke to my heart and said, "I want you to know—
You will be at peace once you release and let it go."

I wanted to do the right thing because God's message was clear.
But as Satan often does, He kept whispering in my ear.
The weight of my bitterness hung like a noose around my neck.
God's words came back to me to put me in check.
My heart said yes but my head said *no*
Because I just wasn't ready to release and let it go.

Doesn't this sound familiar, so much like many of us today?

Forgiveness can be difficult when we want to handle things our own way.

Burdens will be lifted and with time you'll come to know

If you want to experience peace—
It's best to release and let it go.

Due Process

Don't stop believing what God's promised will come to pass.

Most times we'll have to go through God's master class.

The prep school has classes of faith, obedience, and hard knocks.

The lessons are designed to enable us to handle any stumbling blocks.

Our thoughts are like seeds, the process may be slow—
But if it's planted and saturated in the Word of God—
It will take root and grow.

At times it may seem God has forgotten because the process

Is taking too long. But you can't hurry its growth—
If you want the results to be sturdy and strong.

For you see, God's thoughts are not our thoughts
And neither are His ways. He prepares us to weather any storms—

We'll have to face in the coming days.

So keep trusting, praying, and believing
And like the sand in the hourglass—
Slowly but surely in this due time—
What God has promised will come to pass.

Fail to Succeed

Never allow the fear of failure to prevent you from trying new things.

Imagine the satisfaction the accomplishment brings.

Learn to take failure to heart by doing what it takes to discover what went wrong and learn from your mistakes. Failure is disappointing but it can be just the push we need to put us on the right path along our journey to succeed.

Our Past

There are those who think bringing up our past is perfectly okay. They master in reminding us who we were back in the day. In the past, we all have done things for which we're not proud. Sometimes the guilt hangs over us like that of a dark cloud. God loves us unconditionally. He forgives and continues to bless. The book of Isaiah reminds us He casts our sins in the sea of forgetfulness. So when the enemy reminds you of your past and keeps throwing it up in your face, remind him it's covered under the blood and I'm forgiven by God's grace.

Don't Give Up

God is working on your behalf
Though you may not see it now,
You may be asking the question—
"Lord, when and how?"
But like pieces to a puzzle
Neatly put into place—
God is piecing together your outcome
You will make it by His grace.
Hold on to His promises you may have heard or read
God keeps His word and will do exactly what He said.
All He requires is that you do your part.
Simply trust His plan and don't lose heart.
Though you're in a holding pattern,
The end results may look slim—
Hold on and keep the faith—
And don't you dare give up on Him!

Accept What God Allows

Accept what God allows despite what we're going through. Sometimes hope is all we have to hold on to. Accept what God allows without hesitation despite not having an answer or explanation. Accept what God allows though we may not understand. We must accept His will when things don't go as planned. Learn to accept what God allows because as children of His—sometimes we must face the fact—it is what it is.

Never Stop Believing

Never stop believing in the power of prayer, knowing that God will meet us there. Never stop believing in the power of hope. Especially when it seems we're at the end of our rope. Never stop believing in the power of love, something that seems to be too little of. Never stop believing in the power within, knowing with faith—we can win. Sometimes we need something to hold onto. Those times we're confused and don't quite know what to do. Just know our faith will see us through, so never stop believing.

This Too Shall Pass

Behind every dark cloud is a silver lining. No need to complain so stop your whining. Let your worries fade away like withered grass. Stop and realize this too shall pass. Some problems can bring us to our knees because we can't see the forest for the trees. There are lessons to be learned in life's master class, but just know in due time, this too shall pass. What we've gone through has made us who we are today. Despite any mistakes we've made along the way. Our dreams may seem shattered like pieces of broken glass but have faith to believe this too shall pass.

Victorious

We are victories—a *vessel* created from the dust of the earth. We are victorious; we have *value*—a precious jewel of great worth. We are victorious and not a *victim* of our present circumstance. We are victorious and speak *volume*. Praise God for another chance. Jesus paid an awesome price. When He made the ultimate sacrifice. Because of sin's debt, paid at Calvary, praise be to God, we have the victory!

On a Hill Called Calvary

I was the defendant, justice was waiting to decide my case. I was guilty as charged; the death penalty I stood to face. But Grace intervened in my behalf and said, "My child, you've been set free." Your debt was paid long ago on a hill called Calvary.

When Mercy signed the release papers, Grace posted my bail. Jesus going to that old rugged cross, saved my soul from a burning hell. His death, burial, and resurrection is my "assurance" policy. That my sin debt was stamped Paid in Full on a hill called Calvary.

Now I'm on spiritual probation, God's keeping a record of all I say and do. Lord, help me commit to doing the things that are most pleasing unto you. How well we live here on earth determines where we'll spend eternity. And I owe it all to the love Jesus displayed—on a hill called Calvary!

Spiritual Maintenance

The Bible, our operator's manual, was written for our protection. It provides us with instructions for spiritual maintenance direction.

Heaven is our dealership, God is the head mechanic. If our parts aren't working properly, there's no need to panic.

Any parts that the dealership has to rebuild or replace, we have a lifetime warranty, which is God's amazing grace!

If we're not seeking God's direction, we must bear in mind—we need to return to the dealership and have our "wills" aligned.

Spiritual engine won't crank? Check to see if the battery's dead. You just might need the Holy Spirit to "recharge" you instead.

Just as our cars have to be serviced, spiritually our lives need servicing too. So that we may properly perform the job, God has assigned us to do!

God Answers Prayers

We ask God for so many things, and oftentimes we find God doesn't always grant our requests because He has a greater purpose in mind.

Some of our wants would be harmful, so therefore God has to say no. Other times He tells us to wait because He knows we need to grow.

Sometimes we are impatient, other times we become upset. Feeling that God has forgotten because we haven't received an answer yet.

But God, who's all wise and all knowing, is deserving of our trust. He has a divine plan and knows what's best for us.

So if you've asked God for something special, just be aware, though you may not receive the expected response, God will hear and answer your prayer!

God Keeps Making a Way for Me

A sinner saved by grace, a diamond in the rough, I was brought up in the church, but just going is not enough. God is chiseling my rough places, I'm not all that I should be, but the *divine craftsman* just keeps on making a way for me.

Like any wayward sheep, at times we go astray. With the carnal mind, we want to do things our own way. But when I came to know the Shepherd, David refers to us in Psalm 23—my constant *guide and protector keeps making a way for me!*

Sometimes we are too comfortable and become too at ease. Every now and then God has to "shake us up," bringing us to our knees. The trials and storms we encounter are designed to make us strong you see—my *shelter* in times of storm just keeps making a way for me!

The things I've experienced in life, God has worked them for my good. Though at times I haven't always done everything I should. If it wasn't for God's grace and mercy, sometimes I wonder where I'd be—my *rock and strong* tower just keeps making a way for me!

Spiritual Growth

A seed planted in soil must die before it can grow. After a heavy downpour, we see a colorful rainbow.

Once a flower is crushed, the fragrance is at its best. Every problem we encounter, we're being put to a test.

God's working through our trials to get the best service out of us. In hopes that He will gain our complete faith and trust.

So whatever circumstance you may be going through, just be reassured—a greater blessing is in store for you!

Fair Weather Excuses

In *January* we promised the Lord, "I'm gonna do better this year." But once *February* rolls around, our resolutions don't seem quite sincere. *March* is such a tricky month, "Unpredictable weather is such a pain." *April,* we have yet another excuse, "Child, it's just too much rain." *May* ushers in warm weather, "It's time to get out and have some fun." *June,* "I'm going on vacation, to relax and soak up a little sun." *July,* the perfect month for picnics and family barbeques as a rule. *August,* "I can't believe it's time for the children to go back to school." *September,* "I can't possibly miss my favorite teams playing football." *October,* "It's getting a little chilly now, that's to be expected now that it's fall." *November,* "I'm getting ready for Thanksgiving, I've got to prepare my turkey with dressing, and sweet potato pie." *December,* "There's just so much to do before Christmas, so many presents I have to buy."

Yes, as another year rapidly comes to a close what we haven't accomplished becomes quite clear. But we'll sum it all up and brush it off by saying, "Well, Lord, I'll just try to do better next year!"

Parents' Revenge

Children refer to their parents as being "old-fashioned" and feel what it's like to be young; they couldn't possibly know. But their attitudes won't change until experience allows them to mature and grow.

The things we were scolded and punished for because we wanted to do things our own way are the very things we may later regret and, through our children, have to reap someday.

The things our parents insisted we do and we asked the question why—upon becoming a parent their guidance and wisdom we'll learn to rely.

For as you leave you parents' nest and are no longer under their wings, the way your parents reared you—with your children you'll find yourself doing some of the very same things.

So when your children tend to rebel and go through that "know it all" phase, your chance as parents to get even will come through the "little ones" they'll have to raise!

Letting Go

There comes a time in life when parents must let their children go. You've nurtured and cared for them and, through the years, watched them grow.

But once they become adults, there are choices they will make that parents may not always approve of, but it's the direction they've chosen to take.

Be patient and understanding, reassuring them you are there. Whether to offer advice or a listening ear—children need to know you care.

Don't be too critical or judgmental, for as children grow older, they will learn you weren't trying to run their lives—that was just your way of showing concern.

Children grow up so quickly, but in time, you will come to know that a major step in parenting begins with—letting your children go!

Special People

Some folk have that special touch that makes the day seem worthwhile. It's in the cheerfulness of their voice or through the expressions of their smile.

Some folk have that special knack of knowing what to say. Words of wisdom to inspire us in a very positive way.

Some folk have that special gift of just being there. To listen or offer a word of advice that lets you know they truly care.

I thank God for the special people who encouraged and believed in me. Words cannot fully express just how grateful I'll always be!

About the Author

Ilene Rowser has been in the medical billing profession for over thirty-five years. However, her true passion is writing, which she has been doing for over thirty years. It is her desire that something read or said will encourage, motivate, and inspire you in your daily walk with the Lord.

CPSIA information can be obtained
at www.ICGtesting.com
Printed in the USA
LVHW030148291220
675306LV00006B/374

9 781098 059163